DATE DUE

DE 16 '94			

DEMCO 38-296

Frost on the Window

By the same author

Mary Stewart's Merlin Trilogy
The Crystal Cave
The Hollow Hills
The Last Enchantment

Thornyhold
The Wicked Day
Touch Not the Cat
The Gabriel Hounds
Airs Above the Ground
This Rough Magic
The Moon-Spinners
The Ivy Tree
Wildfire at Midnight
My Brother Michael
Nine Coaches Waiting
Thunder on the Right
Madam, Will You Talk

For Children

A Walk in Wolf Wood
Ludo and the Star Horse
The Little Broomstick

Frost on the Window
Poems by Mary Stewart

William Morrow and Company, Inc.
New York

First published in Great Britain in 1990 by Hodder & Stoughton, Ltd.

"Cain," "Lucifer," "Lucifer Outcast," and "The Wild Swan" were first published in the *Durham University Journal*.

Line drawings by Gavin Rowe

Library of Congress Cataloging-in-Publication Data

Stewart, Mary, 1916-
   p. cm.
  Frost on the window : poems / by Mary Stewart.
  ISBN 0-688-10541-6
  I. Title.
  PR6069.T46F76 1991
  821'.914—dc20
                                90-26151
                                  CIP

Printed in the United States of America

First U.S. Edition

1 2 3 4 5 6 7 8 9 10

To my Husband,
Frederick Henry Stewart,
with love

Contents

Foreword

It is said that poets, like mathematicians, must be young. And as a young poet once wrote: "If poetry comes not as naturally as leaves to a tree, it had better not come at all."

I wrote a great deal of verse when I was young, and it did come as naturally as leaves to a tree. That does not imply (nor did Keats mean it to imply) that it was not technically hard work, but rather that I did tend in youth to think in terms of poetry, to shape life in those terms, catching things seen and heard in imagery, as a painter sees the surrounding world in his own terms of colour and form.

The poems lay forgotten for many years, and only lately did I begin to wonder if I should make some attempt to preserve them, if somewhere I might have written a few lines that would be worth keeping. So I have put together some of the verses of youth. Most of them were written before the 'fifties; only the verses written for my Merlin trilogy were products of the modern age, and thankfully – because of the period when they were supposed to be written – I was able to abandon the difficult disciplines of rhyme and rhythm, the "incantatory" power which I still believe to be the main striking-power or weapon of poetry.

Here they are, and if after all my name is only writ in water, I could not be in better company.

Mary Stewart

Frost on the Window

The Circle

I cut my finger on a thorn,
  Drew a circle with the blood,
Traced it round a-widdershins,
  Then silent in the middle stood.

Came a maiden tall and fair,
  Passing fair to look upon;
Came, and wept, and as I looked,
  Lo, the lovely maid was gone!

Came another, fairer yet,
  Sea-green eyes and hair like mist;
Like a wraith she poised, and smiled,
  And vanished when I would have kissed.

I leaned from out the circle-charm,
  Plucked a bulrush from the stream,
Split it. There a maiden stood,
  Lovely as a moon-mad dream.

The blood upon my finger dried;
  The maiden smiled, and made to stay;
But I from out the circle stept,
  And laughed, and went upon my way.

The Poet's Dream

I rode across the river
That flows beyond the world,
To where the four red peacocks sit,
Crouching with feathers furled;
And from the depths of water
Where daylight drowns and dies,
Their emerald shadows stretch and peer
With golden-shuttered eyes.

I saw the trees of darkness
That whisper as they grow;
I saw beneath them, staring,
Twelve golden eyes aglow;
I saw the dead Queen's lover
Moving as in a swoon;
I saw a naked madman leap
And laugh upon the moon.

I heard the stardew spatter
On grey grass stiff with rime;
I saw the nine great angels
That hold the reins of time;
I saw the silver leopard
With a heron in his claw;
I saw the cedars nod and move,
I saw the wind. I saw . . .

I plunged across the river
That flows beyond the deep;
I stared with open eyelids,
And saw myself, asleep.

After Eden

Eve sat in the orchard,
And old, old was she;
Fast fell the yellow leaves
From the apple-tree.

Plum and quince and cherry
Hang red with fruit,
But withered the apple-tree
With worm at the root.

Was ever an orchard
Where no apple peers?
In the time of yellow leaves
Fast fell her tears.

Centaurs

Here they were yesterday,
Fetlocks planted in the peat-brown stream,
Shearing the water as it slid like silk
Over the shelf of slate to lucent depths
Where trout criss-cross like weaving of phantom shuttles,
Quicker than mayfly's shadow –

Four of them, chestnut, grey, and sorrel-brown;
Centaurs; I swear I saw them.

Nearest the bank the grey,
Where shadow washed his silver-mackerel sides,
And water slithered and filmed over slabs of stone,
Netting his body with its wavering light.
By him another, raisin-brown, but freaked,
Indigo-barred by the boughs, with girth and harness
Shadow-caparisoned.
But in full sun the chestnut, cannon-deep,
Motionless, save for the idle rhythmic swish
Of tail, and, where a fly glanced, the muscle's
Sudden tremor of light, as the bright silk
Of water flashes to ripple . . .

Yes, they were here; and while I watched, a big
Sorrel, with sweat still dark on belly and flank,
His hair in points of damp, and tail arched high,
Plunged snorting down the bank and ploughed a way
To the sunsteeped pool. They never spoke,
But their mild beautiful faces were still, and safe
To captain all that twofold shining strength.
I did not see their eyes.

Keep close: can you not hear them coming now?
Not galloping, nor with tame thunder of frolic,
But delicately, at the soft pace of summer,
Under the dappling trees.
Keep close, and watch them

February Song

Had you seen the daphne bough
　　Snow-and-blossom laden,
You would never mourn, Apollo,
　　Your unravished maiden.

Had you known the daphne scent
　　Beyond expression sweet,
You would not lament that she
　　Fleeing, was too fleet.

Troy Dream

Strange seas were breaking
  Across the singing sand,
When I walked with Helen
  In a golden land.

The old moon was grieving
  Along the empty night,
When I walked with Helen
  In the cold starlight.

Ah, dreams! might I remember
  What Helen said to me,
When we walked as lovers
  By the ancient sea!

Shall We Mourn Mortal Lovers?

(To Psyche)

Now Helen's heart is dust, and Dido's hair
Bright ash upon the foam
That blows to Italy, remembering still
The Roman's way to Rome.

Now Daphne yields her sweetness without stint
To every breath that blows,
And Rosamund's fair body long ago
Lent damask to the rose.

Now Iseult lies alone; now loudly moans
The sad sea-purple wave
Between the long-dead lamp on Hero's sill
And drowned Leander's grave.

Sing the dead lovers? Should we weep for these
Who loved, and loving died,
When Psyche's lord, when Love's immortal self
At midnight left his bride;
At midnight rose, and spread his weeping wings,
And fled her side?
Love, by his love betrayed, gone like the cold
Night wind that blew
In the long arras, and the colonnades
And empty gardens through.

Helen, sleep softly; Hero, lie content;
Your mortal loves you knew;
But she – on throat and lips and body lay
Only the cold night dew,
Only the dew.

Babylon

(In the month Daecius, 323 BC, when Alexander died.)

A flame snaked up
  With serpent-hiss
From dragon-cup
  Of ambergris,
While looking on
  Inscrutably
From his carven throne
  Sat Ptolemy.

The dancer swayed
  In a pool of light,
A statue, made
  For a king's delight,
Carven of wood
  More magic than
The magic rod
  Caducean.

On the quivered string
  Of a Grecian lyre
Bronze-glimmering
  Curves of music-fire
Flung radiance
  On the serpent-flame
That danced the Dance
  Without a Name.

The dead flame slept
  In the dragon's womb;
The music crept

From the shadowed gloom
In a dying sigh
     Of melody,
And a weary eye
     Glanced fearfully
– As a finger-tip
     Jarred the fraying string –
At the carven lip
     Of the sombre king.

Through the shadowed door
     She stole unseen;
But still at the floor
     Where the dance had been,
Where the Mysteries
     Still walked silently,
Stared the wide, cold eyes
     Of Ptolemy.

Icarus Fallen

Weep, for here beauty lies
With weeds across his eyes.
This fallible thing, this clod
Lies here, who died
Because he dared to ride
Across the threshold of a jealous god.

What is this beauty, flesh?
A net, perception's mesh,
A curious sheath to house the hidden sword,
The bone of bright uncomplication marred
By urgent blood and innocence of lust?
Or is this dust
A shadow over what a-dazzle lies
Beneath the tangle of desire,
The shuttered eyes
Witholding in eclipse the greying ghost
Of the immortal fire?

From the four winds it came,
Promethean,
Spirit contracted to a span,
And lit mortality with breathing flame.
Now the bewildering fire, its fury done,
To the four winds has gone.

The flesh is a curtain, drawn
By the thin, cold hand of the sea,
Pulled and shredded and torn,
Suffering alchemy
In the rich, cold, manifold
Golden depths of the sea.
For the flesh was a sheath of the bone,

And the sword is drawn from the sheath,
Confusion's web unspun
Amazement done
When the last flesh-flake is gone,
And there, beneath,
Its ambiguity
Resolved, lies free
From the last perplexity
The untransgressing skeleton.

Persephone

1 *Chorus*

They say, on a spring day so long ago
Old men cannot remember, that she left
Her mother's side, and went, with blue sandals,
Across the young grass where the cowslips grow;
Persephone, beloved; there she stooped,
Crushing cool juice of bluebells underfoot,
Pulling the long pale stems. The waking birch
Shivered against the blue, and primroses
Stared earnest-eyed; dog-violets like moths,
Like tiny lilac moths, held back their wings
Hovering on glossy leaves; a yellow bee
As soft and velvet-bright as wallflowers, made
In the anemones his undersong.

So long ago it was, on a spring day.

And she had in her look the whole of spring –
The violet's blue of eye, the grace of lilac,
A brow like the apple-flower; like the April tree
Her loveliness of body, and spirit's light;
The April cherry, the wild bird-cherry bough,
No lovelier, nor more white!

                      Could we but lie
In Enna's meadow now, watch, wait for her,
Till the west is bright, till the long tide brims, and folds
His gold along the cliff, and birds go home . . .
But no; the fields are empty, though the birch
Sways through its old pavane above the flowers,

And cowslips are still sweet on Enna's lawns.
And she, Persephone? She sits in darkness,
Pale, still, and stiff with jewels, by her lord,
And violets dim the shadows of her eyes.

2 Demeter

I see the winter earth, grown cold and barren,
Shiver within the arm of the hoar sea,
Whimpering for the warm and breathing kiss
And thrust of spring.

I see the sun let fall the sagging rein
Slack from sick hands, with desperate demand
For a new stallion-team to breast and trample
The bars of dawn.

I see the cities, their vocal towers at prayer,
Clanging against the cloud, for spring and sunlight,
For growth, for spiring up towards the sun,
For time to breed.

And I see souls of men stare from their windows,
Afraid of silence, darkness, sleep, and fearful
Of rest, which they call apathy; making signs
To avert death.

I see, deep in the jewelled vaults of Hell,
Heedless of prayer, deaf to the dying earth,
A dark-browed king, clasping his naked bride,
And clothed in shadows.

3 *Chorus of Young Men*

Send back our spring, O Zeus, almighty lord,
Lighten our darkness! Tear thy bond! Despatch
To the land of cypresses, empowered as Fate,
The rainbow-footed messenger of Heaven
To bring us back our spring – lead undeflowered
Our Maiden from his bed, that she may call
Green to the sterile fields, salt to our lips,
To stiffened sinews, oil, seed to our loins;
So we may drink the iridescent air
Again, and sing again, send back our spring,
O Zeus, send back our music!

O throats of men imploring, blend together
With voices from rock and channel and valley-foot,
With echo chiming from the stony hill,
Till with one cry the earth and all her being
Call her, Persephone! Call where she weeps
Beside the barren willow, where her tears
Water the asphodel, and drop in whispers
On Pyriphlegethon, the stream of fire –
Between the river of grief and the weeping river,
By the river of pain she sits, the river of fire.

Look up, dead Queen! Across the level shade
The stiff and creaking poplar points its thin
Ironic finger, dark on dark, where we
Kneel in the empty valleys of the earth
And pray. Life falters, and we are afraid.
Press with returning feet the cold narcissus,
Sole star of Hell; with quick rebellious hands
Unlock the dreadful gate of no return,
And once more dare oblivion!

4 *Zeus*

This was the best I gave –
Laid life, her flowering done,
Safe in a winter grave,
Stabled the sun.

But fear breeds fast, and men,
Manageless fools, rebel,
Dragging their Spring again,
Living, from Hell;

Forcing to new design
The turning seasons, lest
At the dark end of time
Man should find rest.

Living, he fears to die,
But from this stroke he will,
Dead, face eternity
In terror still.

5 Chorus of Old Men

She brings the cruel wind of spring, to drive
The flowers from the dark, the waking wind;
Lashes from sleep with her insistent whip
The shrinking, fold-winged shoots. Aloud, aloud,
The frozen waters moan and splinter, crack
With agony of motion; far below
From deep forgotten peace, the silver scale
Flickers and wakes to the vibrating wave.
She whips to dance the naked daffodil,
Unmercifully, and dry clacking trees,
So frost-begripped, so bare, poor skeletons
And dry bones of the poplars – breathed to life
They roar and run to cloudward in a black
Ecstatic travesty of flame.

                 You called
Her back, you young men, with your thirsty lips
Agape for love, for life? But you must know,
As we know, who are old, that cruelly life
Is built on death, as the green-growing rye
Spears in indifference from the dying grain.
Love's banners light no skies of spring, for love
Is of the summer's peace, of winter, when
There's time for tenderness. Spring only sings
Growth, battle, lustfulness, the pangs of mating,
Returning agonies of the blood, when limbs
Take weight reluctantly, lids heavy-sealed
Slowly ungum, and drugged sense is assaulted
By scents that pierce like nails, and light's fierce blade
Slashes the eyes. Not time, not time for love.

Go then, young lovers, leave us with the earth,
So old, so close, so nearly part of her
That we with her grope backwards into sleep . . .

Still, still to sleep, far from the waking lands,
And winds of spring that search us like a lover,
Singing of snowdrop-time; still, still to lie
In deep narcotic winter, loiter on
In the far fabulous seas, nor know the pull
Of the fresh north; unheeding flash and fly
In avenues of Ra and Rameses,
Spinning our flickering shadow-webs of flight
Down those eternities of kings; nor ever hear
The high horn of the north, or feel the needle
Flick to its pole and draw our migrant wings!

Oh death, we would go back! To bud, to furrow,
To the very womb, and then beyond the womb,
Where life is a shadow dwindling on a bank
Of fog; no song, no question, and no fire.

6 Persephone

I am the Maiden, the Mother,
The goal, the quest,
Tyrant, belovèd, desired,
The hated, blest,
Who brings with comfort, rebellion,
With rest, unrest.

Once I was child, was virgin,
Free of the light;
Now the high pageant of summer
Beats on my sight,
Till vision flinches and dims to the
Deserts of night.

All flowers of earth, then, I render –
Colour that lies
Aching upon the sense, and richness
That racks the eyes –
For amaranthus that buds not,
Nor ever dies.

So, for a breath, for a winter,
I go from men,
Bound by my godhead to follow
The pattern of pain;
Living, to suffer, to spend; and dying
To live again.

7 *Chorus*

So prodigal of gold the trees, the corn,
That were she Danaë she must stay and yield
To the importunate fall. Now washed in light,
Waist-high among the harvest, slow she moves,
Soft-sandalled as the moon; but like the moon,
Light's self, she treads on shadows; in her skirt
Whispers the poppied night.

So, breath of light, she passes; on a sigh
Over the hushing corn, upon a sob
Of water freshening to foam, the crest
That flowers the rush of darkness. Let her pass.
Gratefully now we drop the scythe, and sleep
Among the drifting poppies, while the slow
Fire fades along the blood. So let her go;
Before her feet, like foam, the asphodel,
In her sad wake, the snow.

The Mirror Song

I have seen beauty, beauty,
  Glow on my brittle glass,
But never today so splendid
  As vanished beauty was.

So take your fill of gazing;
  Time runs, and all too soon
Your face will be forgotten
  As morning forgets the moon.

See! Dim behind your beauty,
  Deep in the mirror there,
Shine the lovely long-dead ladies
  With jewels in their hair.

Oh, they were rich and royal!
  Oh, they were grand and gay!
They burned upon my mirror,
  And died like dust away.

So, be you lovely, lovely
  As ladies of long ago,
Yet Time and I will forget you
  As summer forgets the snow.

To Blaise

(1975–1988)

Old cat on the sill
Sitting at gaze,
Letting the sunlight fill
Your drowsy days,
Watching the world slow down,
Content to dream –
Tell me, old veteran,
Does it not seem
That birds are swifter now,
The trees more high,
The mice more cunning than
In days gone by?
The garden-close
That was once so small
Is world enough, wide enough
To hold your all.

Old cat on the sill,
Sleep in the sun,
Dream, for the golden day
Is almost done.

1987

'Elected Silence, Sing to Me'

Eyelids close in the dark,
 And darkness fizzes with gold,
Catherine-wheels of scarlet, blue,
 Purple and emerald.

Falls a break in the score,
 A pause in music, dumb,
Silence that is not silence, but
 Of music's self the sum.

Frost on the Window

I and the frost have breathed upon the pane,
And he, most subtilly,
Charmed from my idle breath a magic show,
A silver shadow-land of flower and tree,
Of star and stream and faery torrent – See!
Unholy haunted aisles of ancient snow,
The forest perilous of Gramarye!

And all this world of wonder did he make,
The Merlin-fingered frost, the minister
Of quiet, and that gradual loveliness
That dawns from nothing ere we are awake.
A fleeting breath, a fragile window-pane –
And, height on starry height,
Soar the great slopes of pine and fir and fern,
World over world of legendary white,
Where, deeper in the dream,
Glimmers the frozen cypress like a spire
Of cold unshadowed fire . . .
Oh build in beauty, breath of my desire
This wild land, lovely in the snare of light!

Break of Night

The last thrush in the hazel sings;
Dew clouds the grass and milky drifts
Of daisies; brightness drains
From blade and sepal, gathers, lifts,
Spurts upward into points of light
To splash the sky with golden stains.

Night's dawn breaks dim on fields of air,
Sky-meadows blow with brighter ghosts
Of flowers, those spectral jonquils lost
By Proserpine from Dis's car.

As the wind sings from star to star
One after one adown the night
Sky they unfold their orchard snows,
And the richly blossomed boughs
Heavy with glitter, hold the light.

Then shrill, chill, silver through the hush and still
Of dawn,
Winds and winds the waking horn . . .

Where are the heavenly orchards flowered with gold?
Where the narcissus, the starred cherry-bough
That bloomed but now?
Sad insubstantial ghosts that thinned
To bare stripped avenues where the grey wind
Slinks shuddering, without a sound.

But here below earth quickens. From the ground
The daisies lift wet eyelids fringed with red
To the first blackbird fluting overhead.

Repentance

'There's rue, that's called herb of grace on Sundays.'

I dreamed I wandered in an alien dawn
And gathered herb of grace,
But I could find no altar there to deck
In that unhallowed place,

Save where a little fountain slept
Slaked of its tears,
But threaded with the drops the dawn had wept
Along its gossamers.

Then as the dream broke, stark into waking day,
And memory grew,
I rose, and gathered to my breast again
My flowers of bitter rue.

Love and Leaf-Fall

Comfort I sought of the trees, but they stood bowed,
Summer's burden richer by autumn's bronze
Heavily hanging, save for the sudden twist,
Tug at the twig of a leaf grown restive;
Lift, quiver, lie . . . lift, flutter, rest.

What of your beauty? I asked, as their tresses fluttered;
(Light flame-flickering leaf, lift and away!
And leaf-lovely boughs loose gold in spendthrift showers
When the wind your lover ruffles your golden hair.)
What of your beauty? I asked of the trees, and they muttered,
There is beauty
                beauty
                        beauty here and to spare.

But I saw, false thief, how he robbed them blade by blade
Of their beauty
                beauty
                        beauty, leaving them bare,
Stripped branches bare of jewels, and music-dumb,
Note by note fallen as leaves down-scaled,
Whispered cadenzas of gold and scarlet and jade
That flash
          fall
              and fade.

And now (I asked of the trees) what ill will come
To you, to me, now all is yielded and taken;
To us, despoiled, forsaken, desolate, dead?
Loving the wind (they said) we let our golden
Beauty
        beauty,
                beauty vanish like cloud;
But, naked, new music find and lovelier dress
Of wind-embrace, snow-caress,
And budding pains of spring beneath the shroud.

The Wall

I built myself a garden wall
Against the robber, Love,
With rose-entangled moat below
And thorns above.

I planted beds of hellebore,
Foxglove and aconite,
And hedges thick of poison yew
That killed the light.

My trees stood up against the sun,
So black, and thick, and tall,
That safe I thought to sleep behind
My garden wall.

But oh! he stole in the still night
To spoil my garden's pride,
And saw no wall, for all the gates
Were open, wide.

The Music Lesson

Put aside the music
Miranda, let it lie;
Forget it for a moment,
You and I.

Lovelier than songs are,
Understand,
Is your silent gazing,
Cheek on hand,

Out across the garden.
Miranda, must you go
Winging so to dreamland,
While the slow

Sunlight limns your temple,
Pencils new
The tender, more-than-speedwell
Eyelid's blue?

Come, we have been silent
Far too long.
Here's the music; sing me
Another song.

The Wanderer

Now the rich world stands waste
As a broken wall in the wind,
Storm-outworn, moss-defaced;
All that is left behind,
Curtained with frost and frost-engraven,
Are cracks where runes were cut, and the minstrel wind
Whines in them as a wolf whines after the dead;
And the sad wolf's self and the eagle and the raven
Come as kings, instead.

This was a king's room, here where the hearth lies bare,
And the wind stalks in through the swinging door,
But finds no sleeve to pluck, nothing to stir
Save the handful of rotted rushes upon the floor,
For the king walks here no more.

This was a queen's chamber, here where the chill sun searches
The broken arch and the crumbled pillar in vain;
For the bright hair and the white hand are ashes
Long forgotten and washed away by the rain,
And the queen comes not again.

The door swings open, and beyond
The bright ship dwindles and is lost;
But still the waves spear glittering
Along the wake to trace its ghost.

Still in the hall the flagon stands,
The horn with bubbles at the brim;
A heavy curtain swings behind
The warriors who went with him.

And still the rushes on the floor
Are springing upwards from his tread,
While in the bower the cushions bear
The impress of a sleeping head.

The door swings open, and beyond
The bare expanse of sea shows wide;
No motion but the fulmar's wing,
And seaweed ebbing with the tide.

Yet in the empty smithy's chill
The beaten spear in echo rings
Up to the turret-room where she
Puts up her hair, and weeps, and sings:

Blow, wild wind from the western shore,
Blow wild wind to the seagulls' crying,
Spindrift flying, and oh, wild wind,
Blow where my lover is lying.

Lines Written in Dejection

These sails will never drop, nor the ship fail,
  Nor ever the journey cease, nor harbour come;
There can be no end, no rest, nor any sleep,
  No finding, and no home.

I have been pledged a wanderer, for I know,
  My heart can only beat as the surges beat,
My lunatic blood is cold, and moves with the moon;
  I am contented so;

For I am lost, and have no hope of finding,
  Conceived of nothing, and to nothing thrown,
Beaconless, blind, and moving with the moon
  From chaos to annihilation.

Beyond the tide may lie the lands of living,
  Body to feverish body bound in blood,
Where the blind heart rejects – its Self affirming –
  Proofs of its solitude.

But here the very nothing, that makes full
  The errant mind's insatiability,
That drowns the brain, and stays the futile hand,
  And lays the spirit by.

Know then with me: we move from dark to dark;
  Nothing we are, nor can be; this is sure.
Know that all search is vain; and rest, in knowing,
  All-other-forsaking, secure.

Lyric

Dew shook from the wild rose,
Light shook from the wing,
The broken note of the wild bird
Fell diminishing.
'Why do you weep?' cried the wild bird,
'To hear me sing?'

The night was pinned with white stars
Like braids of a queen's hair.
Starlight wavered and faded
Under the moon's stare.
'Why do you sleep?' cried the white stars,
'And the night so fair?'

Ballad

My lady stood at the window,
And a bird sang by the gate:
'Get you into the meadows
'Before it be too late.'

My lady sat at her mirror,
And a bird sang on the wall:
'Oh get you into the woodlands
'Before the evening fall.'

My lady lay in the churchyard,
And a bird sang on the bough:
'Lie still, lie still, my lady,
'For summer is over now.'

The Mountain Tarn

Never lay water
So grey, so still
As this dead tarn
In the hollow hill;
Unresponding,
Still as stone,
As it had forgotten
Or never known
The tender image
Of crescent moon
Or a flying sky's reflection.

But of all that has been
Is nothing gone.

For first and last of feet that have passed,
Every moon that ever shone,
Every bird that was glassed
In the bright tarn's shield
Lies yet concealed
In the hold of the hill.

And sometimes, still,
The ghost of a ripple
Rings from the brink
As water might ripple
Where wild deer drink,
And spectre rushes
Stir whispering
As dead dry rushes
Might stir and sing
And whisper in the wake
Of the wild swan's wing.

The Magic-Maker

Hunter on the amber horse,
  Naked, dark as Hallows' night,
Shot three arrows at the sun,
  Oaken arrows, strong of flight.

From the withered winter sun
  Dripped three drops of scarlet red;
Flung he down the milk-white cloth,
  And the magic riddle said.

Song

I rode alone in a mad March night
   To find if it were true
That big brown hares come out and dance
   Among the falling dew.

I went beside the green furrow
   With the sea at my bridle hand,
And the horse left golden hoofmarks
   In shadow-printed sand.

I heard a scurry and scamper
   Of myriad dancing feet –
The rain upon the barley
   And the wind among the wheat.

A mad yellow moon stood staring,
   And the stealthy sea slid up,
Mouthing the sand like a crazy queen
   Lipping an amber cup,

But never a hare was dancing,
   And never a sound heard I,
Save the wind among the barley
   And the rain upon the rye.

Song for the North Wind

All the sky is stallion-road,
All the sea his beat,
Sky to sparks and sea to spindrift
Struck by stallion feet.

South and south from Plough to Cross
Loud the gallop goes,
Where through wheeling course of cloud
Surge the southern snows.

Sheer Himalayas check. He rears,
Hangs, plunge-of-thunder – gone!
And echo is all that blows between
White mountain and white moon.

A Mountain Bridge

A mountain bridge,
A frozen stream,
Cold moon staring
In a dream.

Cold stars shedding
Icy light,
And nothing stirring
In the still night.

The Shell

(Isle of Skye, 1945)

Nothing so full of quiet,
So tranquil, you would say,
As the still, sleeping waters
Of this island bay;
But echo, echo and counter-echo
Are sounding, resounding there,
As if all the noises of living
Had drained from the upper air,
And from moor and hill and forest
Had rippled down and drowned
In the dim caves of ocean –

All warm and living sound
Changed into sea-cold music,
Broken from swell to swell,
To swirl in the convolutions
Of this small curved shell . . .

Drone of wind and curlew's ripple,
Bark of raven, and beat
Of eagle's wing and wild goose wing,
And thud of spade in the peat;
Lamb's cry and stag's belling,
Night-bewildering moan
Of storm-petrel, and reeds' rattle,
And sunny bees' drone . . .

Voices of air and ocean,
Echoes of living land,
Whisper and whirl in the fragile shell,
This intricate small miracle
I hold here in my hand.

The Wild Swan

Oh lonely swan, asleep on the still pool,
What are you dreaming now? Do you yet hear
The white tempestuous wings of that wild mate
Who took the winds with music?

And will you wake alone, and lonely sail
Curving that proud neck to the wave-locked stars,
Wondering mute to the ghost of the drowned moon,
Your wings forgotten, folded?

Oh sorrowing wings so furled, can you forsake
So soon the singing uplands of the sky,
The glory and the stride of the bright wind,
And the cold north wind blowing?

And can you mourn alone, when down the night
Surges the dark invisible tide of wings?
Hark! the wild swans! the terrible host that hurtles
Across the world in beauty!

Loud on the flying sky the clamorous wings
Of splendid squadrons storming down the dark!
Listen, oh wild bird lonely in the reeds –
Must not your fierce heart follow?

But they are gone! Under the ebbing wind
The rushes take the echo, till again
Along the night you hear those lonely wings,
And the far music dying.

The Eagle

Curve upon curve he climbs, and grey mists slide
   Over his shoulder, swath on swath (as low
   Whispering under scythe the grasses go),
Until, ah, there! he looms aloft, astride
The high blue wind in all the power and pride
   Of plume and arrogant pinion; far below
   Those wide indifferent wings, beats out the slow,
The wasting flow, of human time and tide.

Here down the wing-worn roads of trackless air
   He wheels eternal in eternal flight:
      Always an eagle hunting along the hill,
As long as the moon, the eagle; he was there
   When the first mountains soared to the young night,
      And the last moon shall rise wing-haunted still.

The Peregrine Falcon

Out in a flash, in a matchless dash,
Leap up the steep of the sky!
High, high, oh high
Spring, flinging up and up on the sweep of a wing,
Fly, my bird, my king!

This is he, the daemon, the darling
Of corrie and crag and mountain-space,
Miraculous flight of flame across the face
Of rock; then spurning it, turning
Dizzying up the whirled staircase of the air,
Sure, swift in the lift of you there,
Riding the drift of the wind, your pride of place.
Pure – you are part of the heart of the wind, no piece
    of you mortal,
Surely mortal no dust of you – fierce and splendid, chaste
In purity you and the wild wind dare
Between you seize and share!

Then swing, swing, slow on the slanting wing,
Ringing, ringing, holding the mastered air
Fast under feathers, cold to the breast
Where you lean, rest
On the eddying wind,
Steadying, swinging,
Winging round in a ring, and round,
Watching the ground . . .

Check! Then sudden flick of flange,
Quick, up at a tangent riding,
Glide and rise, golden eyes

Bold on the prey in place of hiding
Crouched withholden . . . still . . . still . . .
Until
There! it stirs . . .

And oh my darling, the flash
Of the falcon rips heaven from the top!
Wildfire whiplash lightning

Drop.

Lament

(On looking up the Bullfinch in Morris's *British Birds*)

Many a time from where I sit
I watched the brilliant bullfinch flit
From fence to twig, from twig to fence,
Admiring his magnificence.

His smooth dark cap, his back of blue,
Wings flashing white and indigo,
The smart black tail, and rosy breast –
What other finch so proudly dressed?

This bird, thought I, more striking far
Than robin, thrush and linnet are –
This lovely bird must surely be
Known by sweet names 'familiarly'?

Laverock, mavis, stormcock, throstle,
With lintie, merle and redbreast jostle
In all the lists; I looked to see
What bullfinches were called – ah me!

'A very handsome species this,'
Says Morris – certainly it is!
'And known,' says he, defeating hope,
'As Alp, and Hoop, and Nope, and Pope.'

Now shrike and snipe are bad enough,
And shag and coot are pretty tough,
But what benighted bird could stoop
To Nope, and Pope, and Alp, and Hoop?

No longer does my bullfinch now
Flash prettily from bough to bough;
But Nope nips by, and furtively
Pope pops, Hoop hops, from tree to tree.

Ode to a Nightingale

O bird of night, enchanted bird of love,
(That shares the honours with the turtle-dove),
Hail, thou sweet singer of the scented dusk,
Singing 'mid lilies (white) and roses (musk)!

Poor little nightingale, do you not tire
Of being credited with amorous fire,
Of being driven by the poet's art
To mourn eternally a broken heart,
And long to warble out your evening song
The lonely unromantic woods among?

Plain little bird (O passionate Philomel!)
Soliloquising in your lonely dell –
Not agonising to the wond'ring moon,
But simply warbling your accustomed tune –
You are become a symbol, and a sign,
A shorthand phrase, (O bird of love divine),
An easy evocation, common hack,
Chief piece of the romantic bric-à-brac;
A storied princess, or a student's friend,
In legend labelled and in fable penned
Age after age, surviving e'en the blow
Of a rude story by Boccaccio!

So, little bird, thy unrelievèd doom
Is, to sing ever in the am'rous gloom,
While myrrh and spices load th'attendant air,
And the lawns rustle with the list'ning fair;
Where silks and satins, lace and jewels vie
With moonlit lilies' rare embroidery;
Where apricots and luscious peaches glow

From the green boughs to gillyflowers below.
Or in the vale of Tempe tell your tale,
O legendary poet-nightingale,
Where to the dryads of the cedar grove
Perforce you pour your passioning of love,
Or from a tamarisk repeat your themes
Before the splendour of the quinquiremes;
And Zephyrs, Cytherea, and the blue
Of the deep billow must be mentioned too . . .

Must you for ever suffer? Can not Art
Compel the other birds to play their part?
The blackbird be the genius of the tree,
The cuckoo symbol of adultery,
The sparrow represent the word Desire,
The cockerel crow with equal amorous fire,
And all the myriad fowls that throng the air
Some part of the romantic burden bear?

But no, I wander; this can never be.
What other bird could understudy thee?
Rook, robin, wryneck, ptarmigan and twite –
Which of the hierarchy come out at night?
And could the silent, scare-cry, staring owl
Be properly addressed as 'am'rous fowl,'
And to nocturnal peacocks' strident squawks
Queens kiss their lovers in the garden-walks?
As well – oh shameful – whisper their desires
To obbligato of the tom-cats' choirs!

Never, poor nightingale! World without end
Thou'rt doomed to languish as the lover's friend,
To sing of passion, and to mourn of pain,
Over the amorous night as Queen to reign;
And every poet, when he tells his tale,
Must turn to thee, poor little nightingale.

The Coy Mistress to Marvell

Had we but world enough and time
I could enjoy your wooing rhyme,
Relish each argument, and see
How you work out each simile.
But, Sir, your verse is full, I find,
Of loving of another kind;
Your vegetable loves have grown
To thrust your Mistress from her throne.
The Grass, you say, is lovelier far
Than damask cheeks and blushes are,
And Oranges you prize above
A more exacting sort of love.
Vainly your Mistress strives to please
A lover amorous of trees,
Who for his solace fain would go
Where Melon, Pear and Apple grow,
Where eager Peach and Nectarine
Throw themselves down among the green.
So pray, Sir, prate no more of love,
Seek for yourself a Citrus grove,
Pay your addresses to a tree,
And *Lemon* may your answer be.

Beauty and the Beast

A Fairy-Tale

The Beast

Was it in a dream I saw
Red and blue the witch's jars?
Red and blue he poured, and full
Simmered the ghastly crucible.
Yellow claws went fumbling down,
Groped for the grey anonymous bone,
To stir the alembic three times three,
And make it thick for devilry.

How he grinned, and (stirring one)
Through the goblin-glimmering steam
Made a sweet and painful moan!
Did I see, or did I dream
How I saw him (stirring two)
Pour the red and pour the blue,
Till over the white of my white body
The black hair crawled like leprosy,
Till dark and light began to drown,
And the boiling in my brain
Like a millrace thundered down
To smash the sense in splintered pain?
Did I dream or did I see
(Stirring three and three times three)
How he drained the unholy cup,
And wound the curse in whispers up?

This must have been a dream,
These dark unholy visitings of the brain,
Echoes of what enchantments past,
Of what spells cast?
But still the fragments of a dream persist,
Rearing a phantom gate, an arch of mist
My mind would shake to pass; but yet behind,
Like dreams beyond a dream there still exist,
Like flying gleams that brush the water's face,
Fleeting phantasmal wisps of loveliness –
A ghostly bird, a broken stave
Sung from a thorn I cannot see –
But all I hear of life, and all I have.

The vision stirs me, and the fugitive
Cry of the bird thrills in my brain like wire;
Shrills, like a far horn heard
On morning mountain-tops, where I
And others with me, centaurs mounted, fly
At gallop through the high white fire
Of morning on the mountains! Cry,
Oh cry for me with your strong human throats,
For a lost memory and a long desire!

In my remembrance it is always morning.
There is a lily-pond, wisp-white curling
To meet the light; curd-cream lily-buds stirring,
Pearled, unfurling, starring the smooth shine
Of water shadowed with iris, gemmed with dragon-flies –
Hovering threads intensely burning-blue,
Shreds of the sky's woof, here, no, here! till eyes,
Deceived and dazzled, combat the asserting sense

That here, and here, was azure's quintessence.
And above these,
Sinking the mind in quiet and in peace,
The enormous stillness of the cedar trees.

Again, it is dawn, and I am turning warm,
Drowsily in the pencilled light
That lies the rush-strewn floor along;
Vanished the moon;
Dawn and the lark hold day in flush and song.
Hark! On the cobbled court
Proud hooves spark, and the bridle rings
As the stallion rears to the bit.
Bring me my falcon, my beauty, my dark
Fierce little death that clings
Fast to the fist!
Up through the mist, my gold-foot hawk,
Up through the mist let me loose your flash of flight!
Wild as wind, your knife-wings cut in curves,
Till after you soaring, strains and sinks the sight!
Leaping the loud wind, still you are keen to my call,
Moored to me, fastened sure
By the invisible lure that draws death down to my glove,
Straight as the winnowing wings of the homing dove.

A world of mornings in my memory!
For ever morning, with a young blue sky
Curdled with baby clouds, the sun
Springing in April gold and red
Where through the curtain of the mist
Red light across the blue is shed.

Red and blue . . . and blue and red . . .
The visions whirl about my head . . .
Red and blue the witch's jars,

And he groped with yellow claws,
Stirring one and stirring two . . .

What do my senses do?
I am adrift and helpless, caught
In dizzy wake of my own thought.
Why, when my mind moves clear,
And the remembered picture glows
To life, does it suddenly dislimn
And, as through liquid poison seen,
Colour and sound together swim?
With sound and sight goes sense,
Slips sideways, staggers, fails to grip,
Clings frantically to the fact of being,
Asserts and reasserts identity,
While hollow-roaring tides pour by,
And from the unholy tumult nothing comes
Except the intermittent blast
Of chanting . . .
And I am back into the hell I know.

Crouching here, slavering to the glow
Of sunset, dare I dream of morning,
(Who cringe and cry at the dawn-cock's crow)
Of young light, tremulous, adorning
Long lace of larches, shaken down
Like flakes of gold upon a glancing stream?
This must be wish, not dream;
Prospect beyond the curtain, where
I, moving white, as man upright,
Blue-eyed and clean and singing, dare
To fling my falcon at the light.

But this is wish, desire born of a dumb
Vision, not memory, nor what will come.
There was nothing behind that dark door whence I came,

No hawk, no pool, no larches,
No glimmer of things beyond the hawk and the lily;
The ordered march of the stars held no design,
Nor the hidden bird a message.
These were not memory of what was mine,
But aching wish, part of my torment, part
Of my toils, the hell of darkness in my heart;
Part of the potion brewed in the purple cup,
The nightshade in my blood . . .

                      . . . My senses swoon,
Drown in the beast. The early nightingale,
Scattering stillness, flutes to the rising moon.

Sing, little joy, warm bunch of feathers and blood,
That will bubble sweet on the tongue!
Sing, little bird, as you have never sung!
Guide my night-wandering steps to the forest bough
You swing your last on now!
Nightingale, sweet to the claw, sing to me now!

3

Cruel the hands of night
Strangle the sun;
The forest folds herself
In shadows dun.

Under the writhen roots
Of dripping trees
Peer warily glittering
Evil eyes.

Over the rotting leaves
Slithering low,
My claws make whispering
As they go.

The Rose

I

Somewhere I heard it, like a shadow, an echo;
Can a dream cast shadows as a song its echo?
Sung to an old tune, a shadow of song,
An echo of dream, I heard it . . .

What shall I bring from the fair city,
As gifts for my daughters three?
Laces and silks and hammered silver?
Caskets of ivory?

So old the tune, the pattern, that deep in the blood
It is known, the question, the threefold familiar answer . . .

Then up and spake the eldest daughter,
That was both tall and fair:
O fetch me a comb of the hammered silver,
To fasten my golden hair.

Then up and spake the second daughter,
That was both tall and brown:
O bring me a rope of the milk-white pearls
To girdle my crimson gown.

O then there spake the youngest daughter,
Was the fairest of the three . . .

This is only the song we know, as we know the carving
On the chamber door, the faded stag in the arras,
The rustle of silk on a stone stairway, the wink
Of wine by taper-light; and the song's pattern
So old – so old it is one with the wind-worn dragons
That guard the gate, with the glinting goblet, the stitches
Of the tapestry's formal forest; only a song . . .

O then there spake the youngest daughter,
Was the fairest of the three:
I'll nothing take . . .

This is an idle song; we need not listen
To the new voice, to the jangle of breaking patterns,
To the whisper persisting, waking us . . .

O then there spake the youngest daughter,
Was the fairest of the three:
I'll nothing take of the hammered silver,
And caskets of ivory;

I'll nothing take of the milk-white pearls,
Though ye laugh me all to scorn;
But bring me a rose of the scarlet red,
The fairest that flowers on thorn.

O king, O merchant, laden with pearls and silver,
Who have broken out of the dream, whose hands bring danger,
I have a garden, a secret ghost of a garden,
Locked against thieves, and watched by a dead statue;
But there is no rose, no rose on the blackened briar!
What should I want with blossoms of satin and scarlet,
Tasselled and tressed with gold-dust, fragrant-skirted?
My blooms are saddened ghosts of milk and moonstone,
Of webbed white petals, shadowy-sheened like water . . .
And there is no rose, no rose, O royal robber!

I'll none of your pearls, your milk-white pearls,
As gifts from the far country;
But bring me a rose of the scarlet red,
The fairest that flowers on tree.

There is death on the rose-tree, death in wait by the fountain!
There is no rose . . .

2

Long ago the fountain died.
The bronze boy with the jar still stands
Slanting a dreaming head;
And at his feet the basin, dried
Of fish and water-weed and lily-cup
Whitens warm to the sun.
Naked he stands and still, with graceful head
Bent to the jar; oh wingèd Ganymede,
Beautiful bearer of wine, why do you stay
At centre of this still garden?
Remember you still have wings, and the walls are old.

But wings will not avail;
For summer by summer to the pedestal
Ivy has crept, and clings his feet,
Green jasmine binds his thigh, and white-beard clematis
Locks her sweet chains on flank and loin,
And holds frail flowers against his throat.

Where water once and lilies lay
The dry weeds trace their fantasies;
Between, in tangled patterning,
The shadow of the briar lies
In curve and coil and labyrinthine barrenness.
By the dry basin, shadow-sharp,
Centring the cold geometry,
The brown bud weights the brittle warp,
Dead focus of a dying tree,
The fixed unradiant point of this strange symmetry.

Over the crumbled steps the toadflax hunches
A lilac shadow, and beautifully the urn

Cradles its grey cascade of frond and fern,
Hoar-fingered torrent of feather and filigree,
With white unfalling foam of waxen bells.
Never a petal falls,
Nor seed takes wing;
No down from the thistle floats;
The berries hang like blood that will not drip;
The sleek-eared lily slumbers, lulled with light,
And the long finger lies
Still on the dial's face, as if it tired
Of tracing out a thousand thousand suns,
And sickened for the dark . . .

And quietly stands the boy, with shy head bent,
Looking aslant, long-lidded, at the spent
Mouth of the water-jar; the sombre ivy
Clasps lovely green-gilt limbs; a feather of flax
Folds its small clear blue star, a drop that holds
Pale mirror of blue's perfection in the deep
Throat of the opening gentian.

Shadows, curved warm to the cushioned moss,
On gentian-tufts and on shut brown rosebud sleep.

Tomorrow the garden to the visiting sun
Will lie as lost, as empty, as old and silent;
The sculptured delicate fingers pause still, and the same
Low-lidded eyes peer down at the dry jar's depths;
The faint flax bloom still float above the stone,
The grey ferns still cascade; the broken rim
Of the pool curve sharp, articulate under the twining
Pattern of bare brown briar . . .

But barren no more the briar, nor dead!
Through springing arcs of thorn the blood
Of the garden's life has beaten red

And bursts the living bud!
The opened casket showers its gems,
The star vibrates, the silk shakes out,
The flower from dead fantastic stems
Breaks like a scarlet shout!
And at the heart of barren briar
Its lighted glory thrills and glows –
The brand where fire itself takes fire,
Of every rose the Rose.

The Kiss

I

Dark, dark the woodland pool
Sucks down the twilight; let me lie
And gaze into its mirror deep,
Till blood unflushes brain and brow and eye,
And the heart slows to sleep.

Alone; I am best alone;
Here where the trees brood big, and forest boughs
Claw down the bending dark,
Where the ferns dip, drip in the spray,
Where the stream checks and slithers, dimples and spears
its way
Between the wet thyme and stiff pungent mint
Till the reeds hold it, and the small forget-me-nots.
Yes, I am better here, for the long day aches to night,
And darkness, on the march again,
Calls the pack to whining heel; too soon
The evil horn of the hunting moon
Will blow cold, cold through the blood and hollow bone.

Better to lie, and let the tide of night
Creep and cover my senses, flatten thought,
Beat to a blank, as a smooth sea-beach is beaten,
As the drowned face is washed into white negation,
And the urgent body denied by the dead bone.
Let me crush this new, this terrible searing of flesh
Her beauty blew to blaze – forget her eyes
And the futile beat of hands against my silent
Gazing; the panic flight, and sudden shriek
Of the blood that launched me after . . .

But what beyond the beast was it that checked,
And clenched like ice upon my brain?

That reined me short, that wrenched about,
And whipped me howling to the woods again?
Am I not beast, then? If I may not have
The small white pride I nourish secretly,
Of splendour beyond a dream, why am I too denied
The wilder joy of the brute?
Each way the other tortures – as a beast
The man in me lashes and rides me down,
While the poor struggling travesty of man
Is beastly rent and worried.

But now I shall stay alone, and lock my thought
Against the dream; I shall be beast alone,
If being man can hurt her; make my lair
In the darkest woods, and when the visions come
Creep to the water's side, and gaze on *that*,
Man hideously mocked, and beast defiled,
That monstrous mask, that twisted horror's shape,
Which crumpled her beauty into pallid fear.
See! Now the dreadful image in the stream
Is blurring, breaking – but they are only tears
Ringing and rippling the water's face . . .
So into the hurrying water fall and pass
All my dear visions, golden noon
Lark-song and lily-bud and setting moon –
They slip with tears into the stream and flow
Together, whirling fast away
To break in freshets and stone-scattered spray.

And I, without my dreams who stay?
All man denied, I cry to see them go.

Now will I force my stripped and shivering mind
Back and back to the witch's den,
To watch him pour his red and blue,
And cackling stir his broth again,

Stir it one and stir it two . . .
Till the sense-corroding pain
Dissolve the final fragmentary dream,
And wipe the human image from my brain!
Back and back, all man denied,
Grovel, beast, within the gloom,
Breathe the choking poison-fume,
Shiver in the squalor dim,
Snarling as your senses swim;
See his claws with poison drip
Where you crouch and watch the whip,
Dreams dissolved and visions gone –
No past, no time, and future none –
Now, beast, make ready for oblivion!

Nothing, nothing, and nothing . . .

What was it touched me then? It burns
Upon my mouth like salt, and turns
The spangled gloom to agony
Of streaming fire! Blind, blind, I grope,
While all denials, dreams, recoil,
Gather like waves, that driven, pile
On those intolerable coasts, where no
Wing whitens, and no foam . . .
                                        Upright
I rise to breast them, and the night
Cracks open at the lash of light.

2

Now in the secret garden
The rose upon her breast
Petal by petal fades and falls,
As lark-song ripples to rest;
Here by the singing fountain,
The rose, beneath my lips,
Darkens and dies, as shadows draw
Softly to light's eclipse.

But in some song-lit legend
A hundred seas away,
Its ghostly beauty flames again
In scarlet on the spray;
Where other visions quicken
The phantom blossom blows,
The lovely flower of fairy-tale,
Of roses still the Rose.

Summer in a War

Harebell over murdered grave
Dainty knell rings,
Robin on gallows-tree
Requiem sings.

Oh sweet blue lily, tell
Why you rejoice?
Why, little burning-breast,
Lift glad voice?
Why not in mourning for
These lately dead,
Russet throat muted,
Hanging blue head?
Make you then, bird and petal
No pretence –
Portion of the turning world's
Indifference,
Ordinance of sun and moon,
Day and night,
That have no sorrow in them,
No delight?

I saw Christmas lilies
Sway on the stem,
Lovely in Herod's garden,
Lovely in Bethlehem;
I heard the robin singing
Near Calvary,
Sweet on the Cross of Jesus,
Sweet on the Judas-tree;
Harebell on murdered grave
Dainty knell ringing,
Robin on gallows-tree
Merrily singing.

Lidice

This is a conquered village. Here is death
Sitting in silence; stone from very stone
Has dropped, and grey grass of oblivion
Crawls in the cracks to blot the lines beneath.
Cottage, street, orchard – blackened boughs uplifted
That have borne fearful fruit – and everywhere,
Over the village that has died in fear,
The thin essential dust has drifted, drifted.

This was a conquered village: but the hour
In which it died brought it beyond the clutch
Of fear, to freedom; and the tyrant's touch
Startled potentiality to power.
Oh fools who did this thing, who dream of winning
Safe from day's arrow, from the noonday's terror,
Authors of unimaginable error –
Did you not know the End is the Beginning?

There is no end, oh blind. Though you have shot
The fortunate men, though girls in different graves
Lie crying through the night, though you call slaves
Children with murdered eyes – yet you forgot
There is no end. Since you have blindly made
Dangerous what lay dormant here before,
You who have murdered sleep shall sleep no more,
And shall, who wrought by terror, be afraid.

The Forest of Katyn

The wood is quiet now, no wing
Flashing, nor birch tree whispering;
The wood is quiet, we can lie
As lovers, close and quietly.
But they lie in the air, and we
Crammed, ugly, higgledy-piggledy,
Packed in a grave to putrefy –
Oh we lie close as lovers lie,
With world enough and time, and not
A thing to do but lie and rot.

The men who murdered us have gone.
The Judas earth is hammered down.
Fretting beneath the trodden clay
In busy motions of decay,
We stir and twist, and settle deep
Into a travesty of sleep.

But not to rest; for we shall wake
To feel obliteration shake
With wheels and wings and boots as you
Come battling the sweet wood through –
(The quiet wood, where nothing stirs,
Where birches grow, and junipers:
The quiet wood, where lovers lay,
And who more secret-still than they?)

But you shall find the ground grows dark,
And the earth whimpers where you walk . . .
Dig. Dig. We are not buried deep.
Disturb us. We were not asleep.

We do not ask for prayers and all
Solemnity of ritual;
But once our pitiful witness done
Let us lie here while you go on.
Use us, and when we have confessed,
Give us, oh brothers, room to rest.

For Louis Aragon

('Je n'oublierai jamais les lilas ni les roses.')

Long dead the lilac, but take back your roses,
Fire of Anjou and milk of Aquitaine,
Heart's blood of Normandy – oh, take the roses;
Mourn not the lilac, it will bloom again.

Find you the loves you lost, find you the ghostly
Illumined missal of your garden-close,
Where through dead lilac and the trodden laurel
Breaks the brave red of a remembered rose.

August 23rd 1944
The day of the Liberation of Paris

War Grave

In the cold crocus-time
  They took and slew him;
No love was there to see,
  No flower to strew him;
Into a winter grave
  Naked they threw him.

Through the long waiting night
  No arm to fold her;
His black and winter bed
  Than hers no colder.
In the cold crocus-time
  They came, and told her.

Be Strong, my Heart

Be strong, my heart, as a beleaguered city,
And guard me well
The gates where ride the terrible troops of pity
To storm your citadel.

Guarded and locked, my heart, but still afraid?
Safe, from your hall,
Hear you the urgent trumpet at the gate,
And winds of pity fretting at the wall?

Be not afraid; compassion cannot enter,
Sorrow is dumb:
Rest unassailed, for here at the heart's dry centre,
No tear, no tear can come.

Unstring the Lute

Unstring the lute
  And lay it by;
Yet with string and finger mute
  Songs do not die.

Gather the rose
  To fling away;
Another blossom blows
  Another day.

How then to shield
  The heart from pain,
Knowing that wounds long healed
  Will bleed again?

To Troy Dying

(March 15th 1975)

Time will run back; in dreams (oh, dreams!)
Forgotten Springs unfold
Long-faded flowers, and we, my dear,
Retrieve the age of gold.

Time will run on, the dreams we dream
Building a certainty
From passionate hope, that past the dark
You'll wait in light for me.
And all those others? Will they, too,
Wait in the star-blown fields –
Johnny and Kim, and foolish Tig
And dear lost collie-Boy,
And Nic, and long-ago Nippon –
Then what of you, my Troy,
Youngest in death? You'll see me come,
And shoulder through, tail high
With pride and certainty: 'Give way,
'I was the darling, I.'

But dreams are only dreams, and time
Is now, and all we have
Are minutes, slipping from an old cat, deaf
To comfort, and too sick to save.
Time runs. The clock ticks on.
Minute by minute the long years dwindle to end.
And quietly, whispering to the deaf old ears,
We let you go, dear friend.

Later we'll grieve, but now, my darling, go.
Find those forgotten Springs, and wait.
Another twenty years? What comfort then
By this black hearth, beside this lonely bed,
This empty room, and all my darlings dead?

Cain

He died without a sound.
We waited then, the timeless world and I,
Where nothing stirred but the rejected smoke,
The bitter smoke of sacrifice that drifted
Heavily on the leaves and the damp ground;
Until I lifted
My voice and spoke.
But there was no reply.

Only his cheek glowed red
When on the altar licked a fading flame;
And there came suddenly, songlessly down, a bird –
Softly down from the lonely blue it came –
And, winnowed under its wings, the dead leaves stirred
As if a snake were turning in its sleep;
And the slow sun turned slanting into the steep
West, and I called his name –
Angrily called his name –
And no one heard.

Sullen the red crag frowned,
With violent upward shadow scarred and gashed,
Brooding over the grave on the damp ground.
The flame like dusty ochre died in the ash,
The dead cheek waned to grey as grasses fade.
Then the wild bird suddenly, horribly, struck at the wound!
I shrieked aloud! The cliff echoed the shock.
The sun dropped into the dark with downward flash.
The purple shadow rushed up the face of the rock.
And alone, as the stars stabbed into the dark, I stayed,
And was afraid.

2

Deep in the womb's dark silence
The germ stirred in the blood,
As the wing moves in marble,
As the fire lurks in wood;

Deep in the moveless forest
The shining tigers hide,
As secret stars in daytime
With the cold moon ride.

My brain that twists in madness,
Hand by itself bereaved –
They moved to the tune of murder
Before I was conceived.

Still in the gentle garden
When Adam lay alone,
The tiger slept in the stillness
As the spark sleeps in stone.

3

In the beginning there was no beginning.
   Here broke a salt and springless sea,
   Here rootless sprang the tree erect,
   The lily knew no patterning,
   The towered cloud no architect;
   The guarded Tree its secret kept,
   Treasure's golden globe unbroken –
In the beginning the seed slept,
   By no Word woken.

In the beginning there was no beginning.
   But somewhere, restless in the dark,
   Disquieting dim Eden's dawn,
   The fire was stirring in the flint,
   The tiger whining to be born;
   Somewhere the fury in the blood
   Against the bone began to beat –
The sacred Tree untreasured stood,
   And she did eat.

In the beginning – this was the beginning;
   The whisper of the blood that stirred
   The indifferent claw, the brooding trees,
   That stormed across the stagnant air,
   And broke in white of the wild seas;
   That brought the eagle screaming down,
   Crowned the mild mountain-tops with snow –
In the beginning, when man dared
   To take, and know.

4

Never to roam again the woods!
   Never again to lie
Sleeping in Eden's innocence
   Under a starshot sky!

O sleep no more in the silence,
   For the child leaps in the womb,
And we wake beyond the garden
   In the angel-guarded gloom.

5

And I, born in the darkness, cried aloud,
Herald of fear, and harbinger of pain,
Incarnate by the groping of the mind –
The flesh-acquired, the blood-begotten, Cain.

Born of the tiger's flame, the serpent's voice,
The restless message of the hammering blood,
Could the sweet valley cage me, where the spring
Lies softly on the field and the green wood?

Mine was the wind-scoured upland, and the waste
Where the wild thistle grows, and the goats graze
The thin blue flower, and storm-tormented trees
Strain clutching fingers down the windy ways.

Mine was the dawn, and lifting loveliness
Of waters, and the tossing of the sea;
Mine the steep night, where the bewildering stars
Light the ranked arches of eternity.

And there I walked alone, but with me ran
Fire in the night, the spark that stung and burned,
Half-knowledge fed with hope, a fitful dream
That mocked and fled, a vision half-discerned,

A gleam beyond the far receding verge
Where the storm-crescent rode the dark abyss,
Light unconceived in Eden, where man toiled
Carefully, to eventual blessedness.

So, when he smiled, I slew him. *Sacrifice*
That shall compel acceptance! Thus the mad
Dark-nurtured impulse spoke along my blood;
And I had slain my brother, and was glad.

Glad, oh ye singing forests, oh ye clouds
That break in magic foam across the bar
Of light, where sightless torrents of the wind
Stream from their springs beyond the morning star!

Glad, oh ye arrowy rivers that divide
With your swift archery the patient lands,
That I unjewelled sorrow's diadem,
And gripped God's final gift between my hands!

Glad – till the air was still, and the sun set
In ominous gold, and the far forest stayed
Its singing, and the stars stepped softly out
To stare upon the ruin I had made,

This white unghosted body . . . Then I heard
Wings in the valley beating up the light,
And hid my dabbled hands, and wept, and ran
To hide under the God-forgotten night.

6

Here, at the world's edge,
Where the big night brushes by,
And over the shoulder of the sea
Hangs the enormous sky,

Here in the bare land,
How may I take my flight,
With only the wind-rent cloud for cloak,
And cruelly star-torn night?

And where hide, in a valley
Naked of bush or briar,
When all the wings of all the angels
Frighten the night with fire?

7

Are these the same rich stars,
Gemming the restless glitter of the sea,
That lit to ecstasy the skies
Of Eden, and will ghostly rise
Upon Gethsemane?
And this dark desolate water by whose side
I stand, amid the clamour and the beat
And crash of waves that hammer at my feet,
Then sobbing wash
Back in retreating tide?

From what sad spring, oh waters of compassion,
Flows this full tide of tears?
From what undreamed-of years
Draw you the gathering flood of man's distress?
Here is all sorrow and all weariness,
The tired knees, the hands grown thin with groping
Towards the unresponsive stones, and here
The empty arms, and eyes still blind with hoping.
Here is all grief and loss, here is all pain
Unsuffered yet by man as yet unborn –
Oh tears, oh music of mortality,
Oh sad sea-voices, mourn.

I lay by waters once in a garden dim
Which could enfold
The stars in sleep, and where the golden day
In lovely image lay;
But laid all these away and took instead

This broken mirror and this world grown old,
And this unquiet darkness deep with dread,
To be my heritage.
For I dreamed once I saw the clouds unfold,
There where the long waves whiten to the cold
Perpetual moon, and all their glory spill
Along the edges of the darkened land;
And like a shadow on a distant shore,
Secure above the weeping and the rage
Of waters, did they beautifully stand –
A star-watched stable and a lonely hill.

Oh sorrowing sea, oh bitter sea, lie still,
And mourn no more, no more.

8

Knowledge of suffering
I may no more lay down,
But gather to myself his anger
Bind it on for crown.

His own hand set the seed
Within the rebel blood,   .
To flower godlike in the shadow
Of God, image of God.

Now is the half-world mine,
We made it, he and I,
And where he built his domes of silence
My wings shall shake the sky.

All thought and thrill of thought,
Passion be mine, and pain,
Till very God be born and bounded
In my narrow brain.

Where the last star shall fade,
And the last moon grow pale,
Beyond the utmost bourne be driven
My untranquil sail,

Till the far limit lie
Charted, its secrets known –
Pain and passion vindicated,
God and I, one.

Of Mercy

What of God His mercy?
If you question so,
Listen, I will tell you
A tale I know;
A story of a woman
And an apple-tree,
And a girl singing
In Galilee.

Gabriel, impatient
By the gate,
Drove out the woman
And her weeping mate.
Locks clashed, night dropped
Dark like death . . .
But the angel stretched his wing,
And in a breath
He blazed from Eden garden
To Nazareth.

A woman sat weeping
By an apple-tree,
But Mary sang Magnificat
In Galilee.

Cain Outlawed

Safe from the lightning-flash,
Safe from the thunder-stone,
God-bereft, I am left
Safe, and alone.

Up through the bare red land
Dark-winged he came,
A sword in his right hand,
In his left a flame.

Branded and wandering
He guided me
Here to the world's edge
Where the red land meets the sea.

Safe from the lightning-flash,
Safe from the thunder-stone,
God-bereft, I am left
Safe, and alone.

Lucifer

I strode along the ringing aisles of Heaven.
The blazing pillars shook, the columns swayed
Like saplings in the wind, the stars, afraid,
Torn from their icy sockets pale, were driven
Headlong, and flung against the portals by
The dread storm of my passing. With drawn breath
And stealthy footfall, that dark Silence, Death,
Stalked swift behind, as through Eternity,
Right to the very gates of Heaven I passed,
Nor stayed until the flaming bars had bent
Beneath my hand. The mighty firmament
Reeled at the shock of blows, and Heaven, aghast,
Stood trembling, till, like the bolt of fate,
The sword of Michael blazed across the gate.

Lucifer Outcast

Now from the blind unfathomed valley of
  Eternal pain,
Let me look up across the gulf of fire
  To Thee again;
And let me, while Thine expiation stains
  Th'assoilèd skies,
Lift to the arches of the quiet stars
  My recollected eyes,
And hear, ah! far beyond the wind
  A thunder and a cry,
Where Michael's shining legions wheel before
  Adonaï.

Not only here condemned from Him, but I
  Damnation's spring;
Sin manifest in me, and pain, and death's
  O'ershadowing.
Son of the Morning! yet from me the dark,
  The chill, the fear,
And poor mortality that shrinks before
  My level spear;
For I am Death, and dread, and lust, war, strife,
  And sharp unrest,
Who once was light immortal, of all angels
  Loveliest.

Ah, might I tread again where once that bright
  Archangel trod,
And put my weary hand into the pitiful
  Hand of God!

'And He Went up into the Mountain to Pray'

He went from us up the rough mountain-side,
Alone into the mountain, towards the night –
A thin young man, wrapped in a shabby cloak,
Whose sandals were so worn that the stones hurt him;
He had not eaten all day, and the stones hurt him.

*

Behind him the lights and voices fell away,
Life dwindled to a point, to vanishing.
And now, before him, nothing but heights of darkness
Where stars leaned through the wind; wind upon wind
And an eternity of darkness, where
The perpetual miracle waits, and morning is,
And God, somewhere among the winds – a breath,
A wing, an echo, an overshadowing – God.

He lay down then on the mountain, still as stone
Among the stones, arms wide, and tired lids
Shuttered against the arrows of the stars
That would already have crucified him with
Their driving nails of light. And no wing beat,
Man whispered never a prayer, and God replied
(You would have said) no word.
So lay he, lonely on the mountain, while
Space stooped like a brooding bird. Then sagged and sank
The intolerable weight of heaven to meet,
In his body, earth; for an eternal breath
Earth, heaven, man, God, locked and identified.

This, then, is God, who, bruised upon the stones
Lies still, while man, the Son of Man, in the same flash

Is master of the whirlwind, free to ride
God's road behind the stars; but God, almighty God,
Lies bruised upon the stones. Oh God, oh Father,
So still on the rack of the world! A quiet body
And a night of stars, no more – but in the silence
I AM, and Alpha meets with Omega,
Et consummatum est.

                        Then He, withdrawn
Again beyond the dark, walks his remote
White ramparts of the wind alone, where breath
Of the world's beseeching mists the emerald sea.

*

He came down then from the mountain, back to us.
We, nodding round the lantern, saw how tired
His eyes were, emptied, all their brightness shed,
Serene. His cloak was torn; he asked for food;
He had not slept, he said, and indeed, he stumbled,
And had to take my arm across the stones
When he came down to the level where we stood.

Poems of Merlin

The Hunter

There was a hunter at the moon's dark
Who sought to lay a net of gold in the marshes,
A net of gold, a net heavy as gold.
And the tide came in and drowned the net,
Held it invisible, deep, and the hunter waited,
Crouching by the water in the moon's dark.

They came, the birds flighting the dark,
Hundred on hundred, a king's army.
They landed on the water, a fleet of ships,
Of king's ships, proud with silver, silver masted,
Swift ships, fierce in battle,
Crowding the water in the moon's dark.

The net was heavy beneath them, hidden, waiting to catch them.
But he lay still, the young hunter, with idle hands.
Hunter, draw in your net. Your children will eat tonight,
And your wife will praise you, the cunning hunter.

He drew in his net, the young hunter, drew it tight and fast.
It was heavy, and he drew it to shore, among the reeds.
It was heavy as gold, but nothing was there but water.
There was nothing in it but water, heavy as gold,
And one grey feather
From the wing of a wild goose.

They had gone, the ships, the armies, into the moon's dark.

And the hunter's children were hungry, and his wife lamented,
But he slept dreaming, holding the wild goose feather.

from *The Crystal Cave*

105

Merlin's Song of Love

The land is grey and bare, the trees naked as bone,
Their summer stripped from them; the willow's hair,
The beauty of blue water, the golden grasses,
Even the bird's whistle has been stolen,
Stolen by a girl, robbed by a girl lithe as willow.

Blithe she is as the bird on the May bough,
Sweet she is as the bell in the tower,
She dances over the bending rushes
And her steps shine on the grey grass.

I would take a gift to her, queen of maidens,
But what is left to offer from my bare valley?
Voices of wind in the reeds, and jewel of rain,
And fur of moss on the cold stone.
What is there left to offer but moss on the stone?
She closes her eyes and turns from me in sleep.

from *The Crystal Cave*

Carol

There was a boy born,
A winter king.
Before the black month
He was born,
And fled in the dark month
To find shelter
With the poor.

He shall come
With the spring
In the green month
And the golden month,
And bright
Shall be the burning
Of his star.

from *The Hollow Hills*

He Who is Companionless

(adapted from the Old English poem, 'The Wanderer')

He who is companionless
Seeks oftentimes the mercy,
The grace
Of the creator, God.
Sad, sad the faithful man
Who outlives his lord.
He sees the world stand waste
As a wall blown on by the wind,
As an empty castle, where the snow
Sifts through the window-frames,
Drifts on the broken bed
And the black hearth-stone.

Alas, the bright cup!
Alas, the hall of feasting!
Alas, the sword that kept
The sheep-fold and the apple-orchard
Safe from the claw of the wolf!
The wolf-slayer is dead.
The law-giver, the law-upholder is dead,
While the sad wolf's self, with the eagle, and the raven,
Come as kings, instead.

from *The Wicked Day*

Rest Here, Enchanter

Rest you here, enchanter, while the light fades,
Vision narrows, and the far
Sky-edge is gone with the sun.
Be content with the small spark
Of the coal, the smell
Of food, and the breath
Of frost beyond the shut door.
Home is here, and familiar things;
A cup, a wooden bowl, a blanket,
Prayer, a gift for the god, and sleep.

(And music, says the harp,
And music.)

*

Rest here, enchanter, while the fire dies.
In a breath, in an eyelid's fall,
You will see them, the dreams;
The sword and the young king,
The white horse and the running water,
The lit lamp and the boy smiling.

Dreams, dreams, enchanter! Gone
With the harp's echo when the strings
Fall mute; with the flame's shadow when the fire
Dies. Be still, and listen.

Far on the black air
Blows the great wind, rises
The running tide, flows the clear river.
Listen, enchanter, hear
Through the black air and the singing air
The music . . .

from *The Last Enchantment*

Merlin's Song from the Grave

I remember the sunlight
And a great wind blowing;
A god who answered me,
Leaning out from the high stars;
A star that shone for me,
A voice that spoke to me,
A shield that sheltered me;
And a clear way to the gate
Where they wait for me,
Where surely they wait for me?

The day wanes,
The wind dies.
They are gone, the bright ones.
Only I remain.

What use to call to me
Who have neither shield nor star?
What use to kneel to me
Who am only the shadow
Of his shadow,
Only the shadow
Of a star that fell
Long ago.

from *The Last Enchantment*